# Don't Wait to Live… Live Now!

By
Shontelle Mixon

Published by Shontelle Mixon

Copyright © 2019 by Shontelle Mixon

ISBN: 978-1-7017-8591-5



**Editorial Contribution and Book Design:**

Bridgette Moody-Bridgette Moody Consulting/
www.bridgettemoody.com
bridgette@bridgettemoody.com

**Cover Graphics & Design:**
Adrienne Brown: distinguishdesingz@gmail.com

**Photo courtesy of** Butch McCrackin Photography

**Printed in the United States of America**
Library of Congress Literary Work
No: 1-8200202281

Shontelle Mixon:
Email: smixon@justasprinklefilledpurpose.com

# ACKNOWLEDGEMENTS

I am so grateful to God, who is the head of my life, for his goodness and the ability given to me to share my heart in this written work. I would like to thank my girls, family and friends for their support and inspiration while writing my first book. Thank you so much to all who helped and contributed to make this project possible. I'm particularly thankful for the people and experiences that enabled me to wake up and see the changes I needed to seize my joy back.

# FOREWORD

"When work slows up…" "When I lose 30 pounds…" "When I find a husband…" These "when" statements for me were always followed by the word "I'll…" and continued with some promise to myself to do something on my bucket list… "travel more," "learn to scuba dive," "write my first screenplay." But the conditions I set rarely came to fruition… work never slowed up. I lost, regained, lost, and regained the same 30 pounds, not leaving me enough time in between to check off anything from that bucket list. And I rarely had time for that screenplay. I was busy talking and not doing, hoping and not expecting, waiting and not living. It wasn't until I forced myself to live now, did things start to change in my life.

Before this change, I was no bum by any means. I was a Vice President at a public relations agency. I had the nice condo in the cool neighborhood, and the car I always wanted. Things were looking up, but my spirit felt down.
No matter how far I climbed, nothing was satisfying, which was surprising since I had gotten all the things, I had mapped out to achieve back in my twenties, when the world seemed to be my oyster. But I seemed to forget, somewhere in those twenties, that I also lost the core of who I was. I pushed

down my true desires. I switched from being a theater major to communications out of fear. I went into public relations instead of pursuing a career in Hollywood because of fear. Fear gave me new goals, so no wonder when I reached them, they felt unsatisfying. It wasn't until my mid 30's, that I started to reevaluate my path. I played this game with myself… what would 80-year-old me think of my life? After playing this game, I realized… My 80-year-old self would've cursed me out! She would've asked, "Why did you waste the real talent you knew you already had?" "Why did you wait to go to Hawaii on your honeymoon when you could afford to go with a friend, a boyfriend, or by yourself?" "Why did you not squeeze yourself into that scuba suit? The fish won't judge you." "Why, why, why?!" It occurred to me that I really pissed 80-year-old me off!

So, with some thought and planning (but not enough to make me feel 100% comfortable because THAT would have led to more waiting and not living), I applied to UCLA film school and eventually got in. I quit my job, moved from Chicago to Los Angeles to live off student loans, knowing that the UCLA program was full-time and would force me to go all in. And all in I went. As a result, I got more back than I ever expected.

I made that big move eight years ago and I'm happy to report that within three years, I sold my first comedy pilot script to HBO. Even though that show wasn't green lit to series, three years after that, I got my first job writing on the hit Netflix series "13 Reasons Why," where I worked for two seasons. And most recently, I was blessed enough to debut my own TV comedy that I created called "Bigger," on BET's streaming network.

NONE of this could have happened if I had not made that crucial decision to live NOW, decide NOW, make a move NOW. So, that's what I'm saying to you. See each daily devotion in this book as one step towards what's at the top of that staircase— freedom, joy… up there is the REAL YOU! Why would you wait to meet her/him? When you stop waiting and start living, you come to find that it was the real you who was up there the whole time… waiting for you.

**Felischa Marye**
*TV Writer/Producer*

x

# CONTENTS


Introduction: -1

Day 1: Ouch "That" Does not Feel Good - 5

Day 2: Life Does Not Have a Remote Control - 9

Day 3: The Power of a Good Meal -13

Day 4: Teamwork is the Best Work - 17

Day 5: We are all Special to Someone, but do We Know it -19

Day 6: Why not A Phone Call or Visit - 23

Day 7: It's Always Something- 27

Day 8: Laughing Consistently Works - 31

Day 9: Free to Be Me - 35

Day 10: Even Spinning Tops Stop- 39

Day 11: Do you Know Your Organic Roots- 43

Day 12: Non-Organic Roots are as Essential as Organic

Roots- 47

Day 13: The Beauty of Surrendering to Emotions- 51

Day 14: Why not Simple? - 55

Day 15: Is Your List Full of Joy or Just Stuff - 59

Day 16: If Not Now, Then When - 61

Day 17: Are you in Costume More than You would Like to Admit - 65

Day 18: Better Late Than Never - 69

Day 19: Joy Comes from Within - 73

Day 20: Valleys are Tilling the Soil for Flowers to Bloom -77

Day 21: Where is the "Social" in Social Media? -81

Day 22: Aww Shucks -85

Day 23: Procrastination Paralysis - 87

Day 24: Own your Affirmations and Compliments- 91

Day 25: Your No's Are Also Blessings -95

Day 26: Success…FULL - 97

Day 27: Ride the Waves - 99

Day 28: Surrender - 101

Day 29: Pictures Tell it All - 105

Day 30: Start Over -107

Final Golden Nuggets - 111

About the Author – 115

# Don't Wait to Live…
# Live Now!

# INTRODUCTION

This book is for anyone finding themselves in a moment when the path is not so clear. They cannot understand the path they have chosen or cannot determine how they got here. As I approached a moment in my life when everything around me was changing, I decided to do something I would have never done 10 years ago. I quit a job without a job. Who does that, right? Well, I did it and it felt like the best decision that I had made in the last eight years. I felt such a peace sitting in my car of the company parking lot waiting to pull out for the last time. I remember that peace so well…it is when I have felt I made the right decision.  I had come to a place in my life where nothing felt good. Nothing felt familiar. Nothing felt happy. The big decision came right after receiving some life-threatening news from my physician.

I decided to think about what makes me happy. What do I treasure? What am I consistently ecstatic about? As a mom, of course, the first thing that came to mind was my girls but I quickly realized I will be an empty nester very soon so my sustainable happiness could not just be about them, it had to be about me.  I am sad to say I did not have an answer. For the first time in my life, the problem solver  did not  have  a  solution.  This  was terrifying! Somedays I could barely think about getting out of bed let alone brushing my teeth. After I gave my body time to rest, I slowly but surely began to think about being happy again. I started using the same words I tell my daughters - "When you are having a good time? When it does not  feel like work? When you could do it for hours? When are you passionate and excited, what is "that"? As I peeled back these layers, it was scary yet invigorating because I did not let myself seep back into my old ways of thinking or feeling failure for leaving my job without a job. I accepted this moment of not knowing what is next.   I allowed myself to feel EVERY emotion along the way. It did not feel good, but it did feel refreshing.

I could finally tell myself that I am not happy. I do not like how certain situations or people make me feel. I liked this path of more freedom. I started with my gratitude journal because it helped me focus on bringing happy endorphins to the surface. Treasures still exist in even the most difficult times. As I prepared to interview for a job, I decided my two treasures would be, I now have time to help  my  oldest daughter prepare for college and to find the career I love with people who have similar visions and servant hearts as me.

These two treasures kept me focused and deliberate in

conversations and interviews I would seriously pursue.

One day I decided, since I could not afford Christmas gifts, I would write my closest family and friends a daily journal about what I treasure. This daily journal then became the foundation of this inspirational book. It became the reason I decided to capture some small things we all can practice every day. I am happy to report as I wrote the last chapter right before my daughter was leaving for college and had practiced each day's golden nugget during this journey; I have started to not wait to live but to live now. I cannot tell you that I have not slipped back into my old "Type A" controlling ways but when I do, I am more conscious of them and can quickly make adjustments, remembering that parking lot moment and choose to live instead. Enjoy…

# DAY ONE
## Ouch "That" Does not Feel Good

Earlier this year, my youngest daughter was eerily quiet. Normally, she will come and talk to me about anything, but she did not this time. Then, while I was cooking, she wandered into the kitchen and proceeded to share a difficult situation she was experiencing at school. After we talked, she said, "I don't know why I didn't come talk to you about it earlier because you always make me feel better." Are there times in your life when you feel like a situation or person did not make you feel good? I am not talking about relationships with people or opportunities which make us grow but those which intentionally try to break your spirit by belittling, bullying or challenging you in an unhealthy way. We all have had those moments.

What did we decide to do about them? Stop going to the get togethers. Quit that job or relationship. Or did we make the decision to look inside and ask ourselves, what am I feeling? I remember the moments I decided to receive this answer fully. I quit a job or a relationship where my season had been long over. I worked through a relationship which I knew would be good for me. I accepted when I was wrong and needed to see things differently.

I asked for professional help when I could not process certain emotions by myself. I made a decision to "do or feel something". I did not sit still and ignore how I was feeling because I knew facing it head on would change my life for the better.

## TREASURE:

Cherish what or who makes you feel better especially those you love. Better is not always going to be comfortable but those moments will make you pause and ask yourself is there something you need to change that will make you happier or stronger. If you do not face situations head on the first time, do not worry; life will give you another opportunity to do so.

## GOLDEN NUGGET:

Draw two columns. On the top of the first column write people, places, or situations which do not make you feel good or comfortable. On the top of the second column write down "what am I feeling?" Lastly, cross-out all of the rows which have continually broken your spirit, robbed you of your positive energy or were not presented with love. Any rows that are not crossed out - write down why you have that feeling, any required change in a behavior, attitude or value which will increase your growth in a certain area, when you will make that change, steps required to make the change and if you need anything or anyone to help you make the change.   When you allow yourself to face your uncomfortable, you can consciously choose to travel through paths to a better you. Now how do you feel...yeah that's the treasure!

# DAY TWO
## Life Does Not Have a Remote Control

My oldest daughter is visiting colleges for this upcoming Fall semester 2019. I am glad I was able to experience seeing the facial expressions as we visited her favorite campuses, particularly when she made her final decision on the University of San Francisco. During orientation, she was so happy to meet people who were like her. Also, she was happy to see where her next chapter would begin and to be proud of the decision she had made. At that very moment, even though I took plenty of pictures, I thought about pausing it forever. I began to quickly imagine what this moment would feel like in three years with my youngest daughter.

When my daughters selected schools before, I immediately knew my youngest daughter loved big and modern schools whereas my oldest always preferred small and family oriented. However, they both loved integrated learning environments. Because we spend time getting to know our family and friends, we begin to better understand their preferences, and which will make them grow into their best self. Why can we not see those quickly for ourselves? What if we had the power to pause our lives so we can sit on the sofa and examine the frame, words we said or did not say or just not move forward at all? Well, that is not how life works. Life has no remote control, but it does have pauses. Do we take the time to acknowledge and take advantage of the pauses? As a result of the pause in my life, I could fully be present for my daughter's moment instead of being on my phone, a conference call, worrying about all the work I had to do when my girls were asleep or planning the next day. I could enjoy her moment and recognize how much I had sacrificed and worked to get her there. I could take advantage of the pause and be thankful.

## TREASURE:

"Be present" in your special moments because you cannot press rewind or pause. Life moves forward and we must seek as many chances to enjoy each moment.

## GOLDEN NUGGET:

If you do not already practice gratitude, you should try it. Buy a gratitude journal. Every day write down three things:

1. *What are you most grateful for that day?*
2. *What pause yesterday allowed you to take advantage of something or someone you could be thankful?*
3. *How will you pause tomorrow to enjoy or be thankful for something?*

At the end of the year, before you start your next gratitude journal, read a few pages of this year's journal and frame your two favorites.  If they include someone you love, give it to them.

12

# DAY THREE
## The Power of a Good Meal

Breaking bread and sometimes libations with my friends and family are always my happiest times.  It seems so small but during those times we often shared laughs, life major events, jokes, food, private news, advice, photographs, games and even tears. I am also embarrassed to say these meals were often not good for us either but because we do not eat them very often, they were okay.

Did you know healthier meals bring us together for such happy times, are less likely to cause us to be overweight, and help kids perform better academically, have better relationships with their parents and engage in less risky behaviors? However, in the past 20 years the frequency of family dinners declined 33 percent. Why do Americans now spend a higher percentage of their food budget on restaurants (50.3%) more than they do on groceries (49.7%)?[1] Why do 67% of most workers sit at their desks and eat lunch more than once per week instead of going out or meeting co-workers/friends?[2] Why can't friends find time to get together? I am not sure there is any good reason except, we do not make it a priority. If I had a dollar for every time, I actually made one of these happen and how good I felt afterwards, I would be a billionaire.

**TREASURE:**

"Forty-six percent of respondents said they communicate with friends or family more frequently via technology than in person, while 26% said the opposite."[3] However, "over 50% of the families that hold reunions have them every year or every other year. Most family reunions have at least three or four generations in attendance.[4] "A family reunion is a celebration of love and connection. These gatherings give everyone a chance to take a break from work and school, spend some quality time together and remember what's uniquely wonderful about being part of the same family."[5]

Simple things like a meal, phone call, personal letter or card help us stay connected in a way that technology can never replace. Sharing good or bad meals with anyone you love makes us happy. They give us time to catch-up on each other's lives. When is the last time you scheduled a meal with someone you love? Do we really need to plan a reunion to make time to connect?

## GOLDEN NUGGET:

Get your calendar and a blank sheet of paper. On the blank sheet of paper, do the following:

- *Write down every person you want to spend quality time with.*
- *Schedule the time like you do anything else,*
- *Commit to doing it and draw a heart next to it as a reminder of how it makes you feel when it's completed.*

When you plan your work or personal schedule, make spending time with those you love a priority.

# DAY FOUR
## Teamwork is the Best Work

Cryotherapy, sometimes known as cold therapy, is the use of extremely low temperatures to reduce inflammation and help with circulation.  I would have never tried this without my boot camp coach and soul sisters.  It was one of my most memorable moments last year because I stepped out of my comfort zone with others I love.  Can you think of at least three things you have done without any fear because you shared it with someone you care about?

Why did you finally take the leap? Was there something special about the timing? Nah. Was it because you were tired of putting it off? Not likely. Or was the price, right? Absolutely not. It was because you were able to experience it in great company.  So, if you have good company, why would you need a bucket list or why would you be putting it off? Nike says it best - Just Do It!!!

**TREASURE**:

Is there something outside of your comfort zone that you want to do, try, or start? Consider plunging into it with someone you love? If you did not do it right, you could laugh about it with them. If you made a complete idiot of yourself, you know they would keep it to themselves.

If you actually injured or embarrassed yourself, you know they would be there to pick up your shattered bones or ego. It is important to have those special people in your life. What are you doing to nurture them so when the time comes, they will plunge with you with no judgement? It makes all the difference.

**GOLDEN NUGGET:**

I am not criticizing bucket lists, but I am going to call them life lists instead. Living now and taking small steps every day holds us accountable to living a full life because it is more natural. We all have things, places or people we want to experience. Pick at least one or two that you want to do each quarter with someone special in your life. The great news about doing this exercise every quarter is you have time to celebrate and prepare for the next one. Before you know it, you and a loved one are doing life list things together every day! Now that's a bucket list!!!

# DAY FIVE
## We are all special to someone, but do we know it?

As my girls blossom into their own personalities, I recognize the good times with my loved ones, both those who are living and those who are now deceased. This year I have had so many moments when I was thankful for the flashback of a memory with a loved one or I wanted to thank loved ones for allowing me to see myself in them. If we spend our days understanding better what makes our loved ones special, think about how much more we would enjoy them when they are living. We spend so much of our days on what we do not like about them and we forget what we do like. How many marriages, friendships or relationships would be saved if we just remembered what we loved about them on the very first day that we met them?

Conversely, how many have been saved because we did remember what we loved about them on the very first day we met them? When anyone I love is having a hard time, I remind them of why they are special or how they pulled themselves out of a previous hard place. It was not because they did not know it already but because they just needed to be reminded.

## TREASURE:

Life is a rearview mirror, there are no rewinds, but I am glad our minds and hearts (sometimes with the help of photographs and videos) capture those priceless moments. We do not savor the moments when we are happy, living or just being as much as we should. We are often focusing on these moments when we are unhappy, after someone has passed away or in the hurry of our everyday lives. I love how the entertainment industry seems to have recognized this phenomenon after the African American entertainment community has lost so many great people in the last ten years. They have started to honor them while they are healthy, alive and able to appreciate the affirmation of their contributions to society.

Joel Osteen told a story once of a soldier who died in combat and one of the few things, he carried with him at all times was a list of the special things his elementary school classmates said about him. I want everyone I love to know how special they are to me while they are living.

## GOLDEN NUGGET:

Get a notepad and begin this exercise. For every loved one in your life, write down their name, when you met them, and at least one thing that makes them special in your life. At least once every year, pull this notepad out, add something else to the list and then write them to tell them since "x date" you've been special in my life because of "y". If we all did this for our loved ones, I wonder how many of our notes would be carried in glove compartments, wallets, chest boxes, jewelry boxes, wallets, purses, journals or diaries. You won't know until you write the first note. Maya Angelou said – people remember how you make them feel.

22

# DAY SIX
## Why not a Phone Call or Visit?

Over the course of this year, I received many texts and emails from my loved ones. You are probably thinking…this seems normal but when you truly love someone you know a text/email from a TEXT/EMAIL.  I picked up the phone and called them.  When they began to share what was really bothering them it became so much more.  I did not have to fix it or even make it better.  I just had to be present.   It became a moment of love, gratitude, silence, peace, friendship and making what seemed impossible possible.

Genuine relationships are those which make you feel safe. These relationships are places you can truly be yourself. They are relationships where there is no judging or keeping score. These are relationship were love abides. Many of us live in relationships where we pour out the most and rarely are the recipient of being poured into. Love does not work this way neither does true friendship. Many of us do not have safe haven relationships in our life where love exists. Is it because we do not invite love in? Is it because we are afraid of love? Is it because we do not trust others will like our genuine self? Is it because it is safer to compartmentalize our relationships for a certain outcome, purpose or season? Whatever the answer, just remember when we rob ourselves of love over time; we run the risk there will be few or no one to receive our TEXT/EMAIL when we really need that phone call or face-to-face visit.

## TREASURE:

Life is crazy! Being able to choose how you spend the next ten minutes is a blessing. How often do we reach out to share with the people who fill our cups, who are always present and ready to share their authentic self with us? If the answer is not often, we are missing out on these moments of genuine love and appreciation. If you do not like the answer to any of the questions, how can you change it? Do you want to change it? The more you open yourself up to love and being present the more people you add to your TEXT/EMAIL list. Next time you get a TEXT/EMAIL from a loved one…call them…they just may need you.

## GOLDEN NUGGET:

Think of the people who fill your cup when it is empty or remind you not to let your cup get empty for those who rarely fill it up. Schedule a recurring call or a time to write those people a letter or card. Set aside time to watch your favorite show with them via FaceTime. Love does not need frills, expensive gifts, or even to talk every day. Love just needs authenticity and time to be nurtured. Pay attention to how much better you feel when you consciously are grateful for one another!!!

26

# DAY SEVEN
## It's Always Something

Until this summer, I did not realize how much I took waking-up for granted.  Before having major surgery, I received anesthesia which put me out cold.  After many, many hours later, I woke-up to my family, friends, many texts/emails, flowers and most of all the world! Now, I think so differently about my first breath. Opening my eyes to my life now had a completely different meaning to me. We spend so much time doing the "somethings" that we dread waking up some mornings.  What is sad is it takes a major surgery or a life event to encourage us to reduce the "somethings" which make waking up hard. What is also sad is we are responsible for those "somethings".

We spend so many of our days doing things we do not want to do, spending time with people we do not want to see and going places we do not want to go that there is little time left in our days for our wants.  We can seize our power to choose more days when we wake up to our first breath in anticipation of doing things we want to do, spending time with people we want to see and going places we want to go. When you write it down, does it seem really simple? Most of us, do not take steps towards what we really want out of fear mostly.

Fear of missing out, of not being in the "in crowd", of what others may think, of not being recognized or appreciated, or of people seeing the real us.  Getting over our fears gets us out of bed with the enthusiasm to not let the "somethings" prevent us from taking a fresh breath every morning.

**TREASURE:**

I wish I could have bottled up the joy and gratitude of waking-up from my surgery to replay it every morning. I encourage you to be joyful and grateful every day when you wake-up and not let fear of the "something" stop you. This allows you to breathe over the small things such as:

- *Seeing your wiser mind and body again (even as they age)*
- *Hearing the kids/pets who will not listen to you or need money/support*
- *Helping the spouse or significant other who left the water running*
- *Doing the chores within in your house/apartment*
- *Preparing a healthy breakfast*
- *Responding to a work email*
- *Working the business with its ups and down*
- *Talking to a parent who is just checking up on you*
- *Being there for friends who cannot wait to talk to you.*

Do not let fear keep you from making decisions that free you to do, feel, be, go and think whatever you want to breathe and wake up every day. Do not wait to wake-up to your life when a major life event occurs.

## GOLDEN NUGGET:

As a leader, I would always ask my team to complete a start, stop and continue exercise annually. We would allow the staff to complete theirs anonymously just in case there was something they didn't feel comfortable sharing openly. The exercise always freed us from doing things that would hold us back or make us inefficient. Also, the exercise encouraged us to continue things which were moving us forward at a pace everyone could live with. Equally, it encouraged us to start things we might have been afraid to say or do without consensus or this type of exercise.

Now that you know how it works, do your own start, stop and continue exercise. Do the exercise at least quarterly to see how many of them create opportunities for you to wake up to doing more things you want to do, spending more time with people you want to see and going more places you want to go. Is this not a new way to look at your "something" and kill your fears?

# DAY EIGHT
## Laughing Consistently Works!

Laughing…my smile and laugh are so much a part of me that people often tell me - "I miss you and your laugh!" This year there were so many times when I laughed so hard with a loved one that I literally almost burst into tears. Those times were often about just how crazy some of the things we think and say sound when you say them out loud to someone you love. I love laughing with my sister who makes herself laugh out loud. When I talk to my great aunt, who is my kindred spirit, we laugh each other into a state of euphoria over absolutely NOTHING! I do LOVE to laugh!!! Laughter can turn a serious situation into a moment that is tolerable. Laughter can make a sick patient forget their ailments. Laughter can bring a smile to a secluded child's face. Laughter can spark up a good conversation between two strangers. Laughter can bring silent voices to an already quiet room. Laughter makes the heart pump faster. Laughter creates a melody in a tense situation. Laughter, like music and if done authentically, is a universal language. Frequent laughter has been attributable to better health and a longer life. I can go on and on about the benefits of laughter, but many rarely experience even a smile a day. Why has laughter gone astray? Become scarce? This is simple.

We have become TOO serious!!! Everyone has become super sensitive to who they are not. Yes, not who they are but who they are not. Every human being is just a human being. None are better or worse than another, but we treat each other as such which makes everything we do, say or think about us! If we are not better or worse human beings then whatever is said, done or thought about others applies to me too. For example, if her shoes are ugly then at some point my shoes are going to be ugly too. If I live this life long enough, someone else's story will become a portion of my story. Therefore, if the human experience is shared by everyone then find the silver lining in it, because it is sure to become yours or someone you love.

## TREASURE:

I heard something from Joel Osteen years ago which stuck with me, "When something is happening, ask yourself - will this matter in 5 seconds, 5 minutes, 5 hours, 5 days, 5 months or 5 years?" Most things will not matter in any one of these time periods so do not get worked up - smile about them. How long has it been since you had a good deep belly laugh? Now I am going to remind myself every day if I am not laughing, I am missing out on the human experience and losing a piece of who I am each day.  Every human being should laugh at least once per day.

If we were all aware and not super sensitive to who we are not, we could just be who we are – open to being in the human experience which brings love, peace, kindness, joy, self-control, patience, long suffering, goodness, faithfulness, and gentleness [Galatians 5:22]. As a result, there would be more opportunities to laugh at ourselves and with others!

**GOLDEN NUGGET:**

Try to practice being open to the human experience every day.  During those times of the day, do you find yourself laughing more? If so, you might also find yourself a lot happier.  If not, review the benefits of laughter list above and see which ones you may want to add to your day. Write them down and decide what you will do to improve it. If it is neither, maybe you need some help finding your way back to the human experience which adds more laughter to your life. Pick someone you love or if you feel it is more serious, find a professional. Based upon all the benefits above and those we did not list, getting your laughter back is no laughing matter so we should be prepared to do whatever it takes!

# DAY NINE
## Free to Be Me

Being a type "A" person, I have always preferred to have a plan, not to the very second but at least the next day. Lol! But with some recent choices of mine, I did not have a plan.  It was scary but also liberating. Liberating because I had options which gave me the freedom to change course and not be stuck in something or with someone I have outgrown or no longer embrace the same value system.  Or spiritually said, liberating because I have the patience and grace to accept God's choices for me.

Rigid plans do not allow us to land in places, situations or with people who were meant for just us. When we create a plan, inherently; we are creating more familiar and comfortable paths.   This plan reduces chances of unforeseen obstacles, failure, working with people who  may challenge our thinking or of crossing roads that question should we start over or take a detour. How does your five-year plan feel now? It does not feel so smart anymore does it? Do you know why? It is because all those chances are the very things which introduced you to some of the most important people in your life, encouraged you to try something new, rebirthed a failing businesses which led to your current profitable business, landed you into your current dream job and changed your thinking.

Each body of water has a natural path, but with a rainfall, strong wind, or man-made barrier, it will flow in a different direction. Similarly, this is why any true zoologist will never remove an animal from its natural habitant because it limits their ability and opportunity to behave as nature intended. When we create flexible plans, we allow who we really are meant to be take form and grow.

## TREASURE:

Make plans that give you the flexibility to revisit them often to ensure they still grant you liberating and healthy choices.   These choices likely mean you are happy and thriving.   The moment those choices do not exist it is possibly no longer a plan but a survival trap. When we try to control our lives with rigid plans, absolutes, or thoughts not only do we not become who we are meant to be, but we prevent others who are destined to come across our path to do the same.   This is what creates the circle of life. Per Webster's dictionary, the definition of a circle of life is "Nature's way of taking and giving back life to the earth. It symbolizes the universe being sacred and divine. It represents the infinite nature of energy, meaning if something dies it gives new life to another."

## GOLDEN NUGGET:

Although my perspective on writing a plan has changed, I still write one down. Writing down visions and goals helps increase your accountability to yourself and plan small celebrations too! If you have a personal, professional or family plan, review them for flexibility. If there are opportunities to make changes, do it. Revisit it minimally every six months and repeat this task. This exercise keeps you honest about making healthy choices and for us "Type A's" thinking we are in control. If you do not have a plan, you probably already apply many of these concepts naturally but could benefit even more by showing the fruits of your hard work and accomplishments on paper.

# DAY TEN
## Even Spinning Tops Stop

Most days our minds, bodies, and spirits are in constant motion.  This cannot be good for us long term, especially our children.  Until I moved to Texas, I never thought I would enjoy silence so much.  Now a day of happiness for me includes at least 10 minutes of meditation or quietness.  Technology has created an unhealthy sense of urgency in all of us. We must answer our texts, emails, and social media likes, capture every moment of our meals, events, and precious moments and make ourselves available for not just those we love, but "like", network with and work for within minutes. Really!?!?

When you look at it on paper, this does sound absolutely absurd. However, this is the life most of us are creating for ourselves, our children and our culture. No time seems precious anymore unless we are asleep.  I do love analogies. I will use a spinning top this time. "When you spin a top into motion, you're applying a force that converts the top's potential "stored" energy into kinetic energy, or "energy of motion". As it spins in its upright position, it rotates around an invisible vertical axis. Tops are never perfectly balanced and weighted. Moreover, the surfaces they spin on aren't perfectly level either.

Hyper physics is the precession of a spinning top. When it is spinning, a top balances on a tiny tip. This minimizes the amount of friction generated by its contact with the surface below it.    The principle of conservation of angular momentum holds that the top would keep spinning indefinitely if there were no other external forces acting upon it. … as it begins to wobble, the axis of the top tilts to the side, which allows the force of gravity to exert a force known as torque on the top. The effect of the torque is to create additional spin while also causing the top to precess "swing" outward. As the top's spin continues to slow, it processes faster in an attempt to conserve its total angular momentum. This is why the wobbling gets worse right before it falls and comes to a stop."

**TREASURE:**

We were not made to function like spinning tops or allow machines to control our decisions and movements. I am not against the usage of artificial intelligence or machine learning, but I do believe they have their place. If a spinning-top stops to conserve energy infinitely is brought to a halt by external forces, do we think not creating downtime for ourselves or our children could become unhealthy over the long term? Machines are not human beings so they can run all day every day. On the other hand, humans need time without multi-tasking, thinking, moving, and talking. We need to rest. The best gift we can give ourselves today is…. silence…it is platinum.

## GOLDEN NUGGET:

Today has revealed the left-brain person in me with my physics spinning top example above but hang in there with me because we are going to use it now. In this world of constant motion, we have to create silence for our spirits, minds, and bodies. First, pick and write down your level of movement – high, medium, or low; be honest. Once you know your level of movement, decide what or who is your conservation of angular momentum or your "why" for why you feel it is important to be "moving or reacting" at this level.

For example, if your movement level is high, you may be a working single mom who believes everything must be done by her and/or doesn't trust her help. Make a list of what "external force or change in behaviors/attitudes" you can do on a daily basis to mentally, emotionally, physically and socially stop to hear true silence. For example, this working mom may decide to decrease the activities for her and the kids to a more reasonable schedule, join a working mom group or ask her mom friends for help. These choices result in time to create more silence for her family.

Lastly, decide what will be your warning signal when you are beginning to wobble because you are fighting that "external force or change in behaviors/attitudes". For example, this working single mom may decide being direct with her kids or staff is a sign she needs to disconnect, plan a vacation or take a time out. Your spirit, mind and body will thank you for creating a life where regular silence is platinum.

# DAY ELEVEN
## Do You Know Your Organic Roots?

Today, we will reflect on family, more specifically, blood family. I have seen my immediate family relationships blossom because we have spent more quality time together. Our family fuels us in ways no one can. They remind us of who we are, where we have been and where we must go. In order to embrace each of these moments, we must spend enough time getting to know our organic family. So many of us are going through the motions of life not understanding the why behind our actions, health, and thoughts because we don't know our family or our roots.

A root is the fundamental or essential part of any flower or plant, but we often only spend time adoring the bloomed part and little time on our roots. We do not complete our family trees, sit around and talk to our elders, share old photos with our children, read books about our ancestors, or understand our medical history or legacy plan. If we know where we have come from, we can better understand where we are going and why we may have ended up in a certain place or situation. When we spend time cultivating the roots, we grow stronger, more knowledgeable and more compassionate about what is required of us during the growth phases. Spending time understanding our roots gives us more blossomed branches because we took the time to nurture them.

## TREASURE:

I cannot imagine doing life without my immediate family.  However, this past year, I used our time together to learn more about our roots.  Many of these priceless moments were during my recovery or while praying, cooking, watching TV, sharing texts, laughing at a story or good joke, eating or looking at old photographs. It is important to take time to listen, share, and pray with your family. They are the roots or essential part of who you are and will become. Create a healthy level of transparency within your family that encourages learning about both the strong and weak parts of your roots.  All of our families have some level of crazy!

## GOLDEN NUGGET:

Consider actively getting to know your ancestors and family tree. I am not suggesting you become a genealogist. I am recommending you educate yourself more about them so you can better understand how to have holistic health, mentally and physically.  For example, if you do not know your parents' overall health condition, you may not know they have high blood pressure nor can you take early steps to prevent or manage it. Thus, understanding why we have a predisposition for "y" helps us make better choices and decisions. Some simple things we can do today to educate ourselves are complete a family tree, create games about your roots at family gatherings, discuss your financial legacy plan with your immediate family, and share the history of your ancestors with your children and younger family members. By doing any of the above, we are digging into our roots to sow more holistically healthier people in our families and communities.

Making ourselves more consciously aware of our organic roots means… we live a life embracing our surroundings and responding more naturally.

# DAY TWELVE
## Non-organic Roots are just as Essential as Organic Roots?

When the line between your blood and chosen family becomes blurred, you know you are blessed. Yesterday, we focused on blood family or organic relationships. Today we are going to explore the beauty of a chosen family or non-organic relationships. Some of us have been blessed with some very strong non-organic relationships. I am one of them. I can share anything with my chosen family safely. I can be undeniably myself and who God wants me to be and they still love and encourage me. They also are not afraid to tell me when I am wrong. I finally have a chosen family that I feel comfortable sharing my vulnerabilities so I can get support and even possibly be a blessing to them. I can even l travel with my chosen family.

If you have not noticed, in each of the sentences above I mention words which reveal my true self such as share, undeniably myself, wrong, and vulnerabilities. We cannot have genuine relationships without being honest about who we truly are, our struggles and most of all our dreams. I am not talking about the people who come into our lives for seasons but those who become part of our fabric.

If we want a chosen family who sticks around, we have to be willing to open ourselves for the relationship or we will have nothing but superficial relationships. Although we do not like to admit it, we are stuck with our blood family, but we can be more particular about our chosen family.  If we are allowing God to place chosen family in our lives for our good, these folks fill the gaps in our organic family's flowers.  I do believe God intentionally creates these gaps just for our chosen family.  The power in selecting our chosen family is we have a choice of who they are-so chose them wisely.

## TREASURE:

I know no one can take the place of our blood family but like me, I hope today when you think about your chosen family, you are overwhelmed by their love and blessings because they were hand-picked to come into your life.  They were the flower petals you were missing. They are people who truly light up your day and make you grow.  One of my cherished chosen families is my female bible study group.  We call ourselves the "turtle formation".  When studying "Armor of God" by Pricilla Shirer, we learned how the Roman soldiers created a turtle with their shields to block the enemy on all sides of them.  It was called the "testudo" which is a very strong, tight formation. It prevented any soldier from getting hurt when approaching fortifications. Now that I understand the meaning of testudo, I wear my turtle shield proudly.  Like the soldiers, I have expectations of my organic and non-organic roots.   When I am under attack by life, which all of us will be, I want strong family roots. We get in the boxing ring for each other. We share our testimonies to bless each other.  We pray for each other.  Ultimately, these experiences show us how to be there for each other and our families because God picked us for each other.

## GOLDEN NUGGET:

Do you have genuine chosen non-organic relationships? If not, why not? If you answered yes, take some quiet time and think about who is in this circle.  Just like your organic family, spend some time with them learning about their roots. Plan activities which get you outside of the normal things you do together. Make sure you think about important things too such as estate legacy planning, wills, insurance, trusts, power of attorneys, beneficiaries, etc. We include these topics in our discussions because we may not have family members who can fulfill these roles or responsibilities. Be thankful for them being able to fill any voids. Opening yourself to these relationships means we are establishing strong legacies.

# DAY THIRTEEN
## The Beauty of Surrendering to Emotions

What do the movies Pretty Woman, Sound of Music, Footloose, 13 Going on 30, Mahogany, Love Jones, How Stella Got Her Groove Back, The Wiz and Pitch Perfect have in common? Happy moments where an actor or actress bursts into a song at the top of their lungs! After letting go of some things recently, I have been able to sing again at the drop of a hat!!! I am so happy to be singing again! My girls will tell you that my favorite song recently is "Never Enough" by Loren Allred (The Greatest Showman). I add my own spiritual spin to it by thinking I can never get enough of God which makes me burst into praise as well.

Can you think of the last time you surrendered to an emotion? I use a good song to express happiness but lately my other go to emotion is crying, funny. I am frequently in tears when I observe nature's beauty driving in my car. Over this past year, I can think of so many times when I cried tears of joy when spending time with my daughters or tears of fear when I did not know what I wanted to do next. There is power in surrendering to your emotion. You allow yourself to feel whatever it brings with no restraint.

It allows you to be present and to process what is behind it more freely and bring subconscious feelings into consciousness. This freedom is what we need more of every day to experience our life to the fullest.

## TREASURE:

What if instead of walking by one another without speaking, we said hello, started a conversation or even made eye contact. Acts of kindness remind us to be present. By interacting with one another, we create diverse and inclusive spaces for safe releases of emotion or feelings instead of loneliness, isolation, desperation and lack of understanding, which plague so many of us today. If we give each other permission to surrender to how we truly feel or to be who we are, think of how we could change the world one interaction at a time. Many people would be happier, more inclined to seek mental health support, try new things, sing out loud, or be present and not keep what is bothering them suppressed or worse unleash it onto to innocent people like in some of the recent tragic events.

## GOLDEN NUGGET:

There is freedom in the surrender process.  Is there something that makes you happy and you have not done it in a while? Is there something you need closure on? Are you feeling a certain way but just cannot put your finger on it? What is holding you back? Today you have permission to surrender and not put it off any longer.  Write a letter/email if you cannot talk about it. You might not even send it.  Call a friend to cry. Sing your favorite song in the shower or car. Make an appointment with your doctor if you've been feeling a certain way but cannot explain it. Tell someone how they made you feel angry or left out. Run or scream to release any aggression. Do not put off surrendering to what makes you happy…if you cannot do it like you used to (distance running for me) then modify it to something that you can do (shorter distance runs over a few days or a very brisk long walk) — just do not stop doing it!!!!

# DAY FOURTEEN
## Why not Simple?

My greatest happiness every day comes from the simple things I take for granted. I am thankful for being in so many roles that allow me to share this happiness and be a blessing to others. In each of my roles, I can encourage and uplift others by reminding them how special they are, why an obstacle is not as bad as they think or of about their beautiful day. Yesterday, we surrendered to our emotions which now creates a space for others to do safely too. As I mentioned previously, I love this oldie but goodie Maya Angelou quote - "I've learned people will forget what you said, people will forget what you did but people will never forget how you made them feel."

I cannot do the things God wants me to do if I am not mentally, physically, emotionally, spiritually and financially well. By taking care of the simple things in each of these categories, I am WELL, and I invite others to join me. It does not take a lot of money to be well in these categories. We have made our lives way too complicated. Maslow's needs pyramid only includes physiological, safety, belonging, esteem, and self-realization. Technology has made us smarter but dumber too. We stopped doing the things which are essential to who we are as human beings and our basic needs.

These simple things included in Maslow's hierarchy are breathing; waking up with a healthy mind and body; being grateful; seeking quiet time without our phones; standing in who we are and not comparing ourselves to others; having choices; eating; sleeping; giving; loving ourselves;   being safe; having people who love us and clothing.

**TREASURE:**

Today was very easy because we all know what simple feels like, but unfortunately, we do not protect it WELL.  The Maslow hierarchy of needs is a way to simplify needs vs wants. Many of us are not WELL because we spend most of our time trying to get what we want versus being grateful for having all the things we need. When we are happy and WELL, we become an example for others too.   Being memorable by others means you make them feel good about being happy with what they already have versus what they want. Just like the emotions from the last day, we must give each other permission to remember the simple needs.

**GOLDEN NUGGET:**

As you can see, most of the simple things in Maslow's hierarchy of needs are almost free.  Having what we need gives us daily reasons to be grateful and happy. Be a blessing to someone every day. Remind people of something simple from this list or in their day, life or circumstances that takes their mind to a place of gratitude.  You might be the only one that makes them smile today.

# DAY FIFTEEN
## Is Your List Full of Joy or Just Stuff?

How many of us live our lives with a list? We create a list for almost everything we do. We create lists for what we want to do, need to do and for what we have not done yet. As I began to write this book, I remembered my happiest moments were always with my family and friends not checking off things on my list.  I remember a time when losing my car in the parking lot would have had me so angry and stressed, but today life has me less moved by such things. When I do find myself moved by such things, I remember Joel Osteen's five- second…five-year rule. Today I am more focused on making sure I fill my days with the life I enjoy and my loved ones.  If we are not intentional about how we spend our most valuable resource, time; we will wake up one day and realize our time was not spent on what brings us joy but on checking things off our list. No list is worth the paper it is on unless it is filled with joyful moments.

**TREASURE:**

Lists should be used to create joy and happiness in our lives with time to pause. Although they are not list, perse; vision boards give us an opportunity to see our lives on a stage. I like to think of my board as another way to visualize what I need in the way God sees it. When we visualize our goals every day with the lists of our joyful moments, we begin to be less concerned with completed lists. We become ecstatic about the path we bring to fruition working through our list. As a result, there will be more people creating their own good news, finding a cause to support, making someone else feel good or serving in their community.

## GOLDEN NUGGET:

Do you have a vision board? Does it drive what you do each day? If your answer is yes to these questions, then you know what a list of joyful moments feel like. If your answer to these questions was no, then you are like so many of us who visualize what we want and let life distract us from getting it or you are like the most of us visualizing what makes us happy but having no action plan to bring it to life every day. In order to have a dream come to life, we need to water it every day not just when we have time. Create a vision board, look at it every day and ask yourself what needs to be on the list today to water. Who do I need to spend time with? What do I need to think about? If you do this every day, you will begin to see the board take on a life of its own.

# DAY SIXTEEN
## If Not Now, Then When…

As we reflect on our lives, life may not look like you wanted. You may not have completed your New Year's resolution each year, been on your ideal job, achieved the status you thought was necessary to be successful or done everything on your list. Some people spend their entire life searching for what makes them happy, establishing the goals of someone else and running toward something they never truly understand. Why do we do this? Our experience, family and now social media, has created a picture of the things, jobs, money and social groups which make us important, special or accomplished.

What about those who never attain anything in this picture? Does that make them less of a person? Should they feel like they do not belong amongst others who are more accomplished? Will they ever be happy? What if we started to focus more on Maslow's hierarchy of needs instead of trying to reach for these superficial accepted measurements of importance or success? Living to be happy should be our priority not when ______. Fill in the blank. Think of how long it takes us to take a selfie to get our "perfect self" but our best pics are always the ones taken when no one is looking. Now in its sixth year, the World Happiness Report is produced by the United Nations Sustainable Development Solutions Network. In 2018, Finland ranked No. 1 and the United States ranked No. 18 — falling four spots from last year and five from two years ago — "in part because of the ongoing epidemics of obesity, substance abuse and untreated depression," according to World Happiness Report co-editor and Columbia University professor Jeffrey Sachs. Through a measurement of happiness and well-being called the "Cantril ladder," Gallup asked nationally representative populations to value their lives on a scale from 0 to 10, with the worst possible life valued at 0 and the best valued at 10. The top countries frequently have high values for all six of the key variables that contribute to overall well-being: income (GDP per capita), healthy life expectancy, social support, freedom, trust (absence of corruption) and generosity. These variables are not arbitrary but simple and easy to work on every day.

**TREASURE:**

John Helliwell, a University of British Columbia economist who co-edited the above happiness report, told The Washington Post that the most surprising finding researchers came across was "the extent to which happiness of immigrants matches the locally born population. But happiness, unlike gold, can be created for all, and can be shared without being scarce for those who give it. It even grows as it is shared." Said more simply, each variable can be attained by anyone, shared with anyone and available in abundance which means everyone can be happy!!!!

Remember everyone learned they could be happy in the movie Trolls. We do not have to move to these countries, but we can learn the variables that make them the happiest countries in the world. If we create a vision board which focuses on these variables and reasonable ways to attain them daily, we could enjoy life's journey with more joy.  We should be content with making room for what is important and being blessed by them.

## GOLDEN NUGGET:

Let us revisit our vision board. How does each space fit into the variables above? For example, one of my visions is to be physically fit.  I have created a diet, exercise and sleep routine which increases my life expectancy.  Another goal is to spend more quality time with my family and friends which increases my social support. My goal is to throw away the resolutions and the to dos which do not give me the grace to make room for the variables that create happiness and joy. Now you can focus on what is important - you, your loved ones and those you are able to bless. These are the people who need your daily reflection on why being happy now is important.

# DAY SEVENTEEN
## Are You in Costume More than You would Like to Admit?

Of the many roles in my life, I love being a mom the most. When you recite this sentence, I hope you are able to add your own role as well. I love the role of mom because it allows me to practice unconditional love and unselfishness. Being a mother helps me see my strengths and opportunities before going out into the world and messing it up. Lol! The one resounding area of opportunity this year was, "make me important, not just ok." How many times have you told someone you are fine when you were not? As caregivers and parents, we spend a lot of time taking care of everyone else.

We neglect to check-in with ourselves to make sure we are okay. We use quick things or getaways to fill the void. We indulge in having an out of body happy experience and never really reflect on what we are missing for long-term happiness. Michelle Obama recently admitted in her book "Becoming" when she stopped checking things off her list, she finally gave herself time and permission to admit she was not happy and to do what truly made her fulfilled. This year I made some hard calls both personally and professionally. I decided to embrace happiness for myself long term.

Some decisions were internal changes, but other changes were just HARD. I gave myself permission to change. Change is difficult especially when all your life has been aimed at one role, path, list or decision. As a "Type A" person, there is rarely a time when I don't have a plan or a goal.

Yesterday, we learned why the USA has continually dropped on the list of happiest countries. Each area can be tied to missing one or more of the six variables or something genetic or scientific, which we cannot control. If we can control and attain all six variables daily on our vision board journey, why would we not find the yesterday's golden nugget liberating? I do not have the task mastered yet but with help from so many I am working on it more and more every day.

## TREASURE:

The millennials, Y's, and Z's have one thing right - they focus on themselves before anyone else. They do not live in a costume or through a list. We play important roles in our lives, but none will ever be as important as the one you play for yourself. Creating reasons to experience joy or increase the level of serotonin (chemical produced naturally in your brain that affects the way you feel, for example, making you feel happier, calmer, or less hungry) our daily lives is mandatory to happier living. Do you want to be happy?

By focusing on yourself, you are happier, more people want to be around you, and you give others permission to be happy too. You cannot fulfill any other role well unless you are happy first. Try some things, such as meditating, exercising, vacationing, and volunteering. I would further suggest that you repair a rift with a friend or loved one, start a hobby, get some much-needed sleep, resume doing something you love to do. Additionally, share stories, sing, dance or just help somebody along the way. You may even want to learn to take a moment in the middle of the day and take a deep breath and sometimes learning to just say no. Whatever you have found over the course of your life that makes you happy, do more of it every day and not as a hobby or break but as a career or side business. You do not need anyone's permission to create serotonin every day in your own life (within limits and healthy ways of course).

**GOLDEN NUGGET:**

Write down what makes you happy. Now compare this list to your vision board. Do you see any correlation? If not, you should make adjustments to your vision board. Now, in your calendar; draw a smiley face next to every task, meeting, event, phone call, or even the smallest thing you did to create serotonin for yourself.

At the end of each week, reflect on the smiley faces as motivation to keep up your good work.

# DAY EIGHTEEN
## Better Late Than Never

Many of us stop living without even knowing it. We stop calling and spending time with our friends. We rarely read for fun. We stop moving our bodies to stay healthy. We spend too much time alone. We no longer plan fun activities or vacations. We only do what is popular or sexy to others. We do not share our life genuinely with anyone; we are just going through the motions. Then, why do we not pause, acknowledge what is happening and hold ourselves accountable to make the necessary changes? Instead, we wake-up every day and do it all over again or we tell ourselves "I'm too old, young, fat, skinny, rich, poor, or something else, but most often we think it is too late to change it. What is too late? What is too old or young? Remember some of our greatest inventions were created by people older than 40. Are you thinking of starting a new career, a new business, or solving a problem?

Benjamin Franklin invented the lightning rod when he was 44. He discovered electricity at 46. He helped draft the Declaration of Independence at 70, and next he invented bifocals. Henry Ford introduced the Model T when he was 45. Sam Walton built Walmart in his mid-40s. Ray Kroc built McDonald's in his early 50s. Some of the most creative people of the century were not young. Ray Kurzweil published "The Singularity Is Near" in his 50s; Alfred Hitchcock directed Vertigo when he was 59; Frank Lloyd Wright built his architectural masterpiece "Fallingwater" when he was 68. Let's not forget the greatest innovator of recent times–Steve Jobs; his most significant innovations—iMac, iTunes, iPod, iPhone, and iPad—came after he was 45.

Kauffman Foundation director of research, Dane Stangler analyzed Kauffman Firm Survey data and the Kauffman Index of Entrepreneurial Activity—which uses data from the U.S. Census. He found the average age of U.S. entrepreneurs is actually rising, with the highest rate of entrepreneurial activity shifting to the 55–64 age group. If you cannot relate to these famous people, here are some examples of common people like you and I who decided better late than never.

1.  *At 91 years old, Thompson is the oldest woman ever to compete in the Suja Rock 'n' Roll San Diego Marathon and the second-oldest marathon runner in U.S. history.*

2.  *At 88 years old, Germany native Johanna Quaas is the oldest active gymnast in the world.*

3.  *In May 2007, Nola Ochs became the oldest person on record at 95 years old to graduate from college when she received her diploma from Fort Hays State University alongside her granddaughter.*

*4. In 2011, Fred Mack celebrated his 100th birthday by skydiving for the second time.*

## TREASURE:

What are you waiting for? What will it take to burn a fire under you? There will never be a perfect time to embrace change. It never happens because we are taught life happens in a linear line and in sequence. What if those above decided not to move forward, take the risk, or be uncomfortable? There would be no iAnything for any of us. There would be no lightning rod, electricity, or Declaration of Independence. All moments are connected towards an intended outcome. Putting off today means today never really happens as it was meant, so tomorrow turns into something else. Our greatest lessons and triumphs come from uncomfortable change. After every uncomfortable step, comes moments of uncertainty and greatness! Without one step occurring, the other step cannot occur. Every person mentioned above was once just as uncomfortable as you, but they pushed through it.

## GOLDEN NUGGET:

What have you been making excuses not to do today? Use Mel Robbin's five-second rule by counting down from 5 to 1 and take the first step to do it instead. After this first step, write down how you felt and the outcome. Repeat this reflection with every step. After the last step, share with a loved one and celebrate completing it today and not putting it off! Going forward, changes will be easier and more comfortable.

Think about Nicholas James Vujicic who is an Australian Christian evangelist and motivational speaker born with tetra-amelia syndrome, a rare disorder (called phocomelia) characterized by the absence of arms and legs. If he stopped before he started, he would not have accomplished so much and blessed so many with his journey. Who are you meant to bless with taking your first step today?

# DAY NINETEEN
## Joy Comes from Within

During the Christmas of 2017, I purchased the book "The Book of Joy: Lasting Happiness in a Changing World" by Dalai La and Desmond Tutu from Oprah's Favorite Things list and handed copies out. I was pulled into the title immediately because of the word "Joy". Joy, I learned is different than happiness which I have used interchangeably throughout this book. Happiness is temporary but joy comes from within. Joy begins with knowing why you exist. What purpose or problem were you put on this earth to fulfill or solve? Until you answer this question, your heart or some would say soul cannot experience true joy. It cannot connect with the flame in you.

During this stage of my life, although excruciating at times, I can honestly say I have experienced the most joy. In religious terms, some might say I am listening to God's voice more than my own. Leaning not on my own understanding…Whatever it is… I no longer push through the seconds of my day not acknowledging what is happening around and within me. It allows me to begin and end my day more consciously and to choose my joy within.

## TREASURE:

It is a belief that you cannot truly love someone until you love yourself. I think the true revelation is you can only love yourself if every morning when you awake, you are able to connect with the joy inside of you and say, "I bring myself happiness today because I am able to fulfill my purpose or solve a problem. It is this joy that allows me to connect with others and love them unconditionally." Remember, only you can own your inner joy. For me, I know God lives in me and He chooses what is best for me. The minute you give anyone or anything the power to choose what you focus on in your life, you will spend years trying to get it back.

## GOLDEN NUGGET:

Imagine you have nothing but Maslow's hierarchy of needs. Ask yourself, why do I have joy within? Your response cannot have any conditional terms or change frequently. If your mind is drawing a blank, ask yourself why? Talk it over with someone you love or even a professional, if necessary. Even read the book above if it helps, then try it again. After your gratitude journaling exercise every day, write down what gives you joy. If it is truly what gives you joy within, it should not change drastically from day to day.

Writing it down every day is a reminder that no one or nothing can take your joy within unless you allow.

# DAY TWENTY
## Valleys are Tilling the Soil for Flowers to Bloom

Until recently, I thought my divorce was the lowest point of my life. I love the book "Failing Forward" by John Maxwell. Years ago, when someone I did not like shared it with me, I did not receive it well but as I have aged; I have become intimate with failure or valleys of flowers blooming. It has been during those times that I have grown the most. I have embraced the chilly nights and lonesome mornings. Those times when you allow yourself to start again and not punish yourself for being in a place you never thought you would be.

On a road trip, the best detours are those with signs laid out and roads well-traveled. The worse detours are when you have gotten lost or decided you will find a shorter path which leads to untraveled and often unpaved roads. These detours are the ones which I will call valleys. Every time you approached these valleys a small voice in you says, "do not panic". If they are true detours you go through Elisabeth Kübler-Ross's five stages of denial and /or isolation, anger, bargaining, depression and acceptance and not necessarily in that order. How many times have you retraced your steps and thought about how you could you have chosen a different path or gotten yourself back to the right path? If we allow ourselves this level of self-reflection in these valleys, the times when we grow the most; why are we always looking for ways to avoid them or prevent them from happening? Answering this question requires a certain level of patience, love, and grace with ourselves which many of us never do, yet we do for others.

## TREASURE:

If valleys are when our flowers bloom, we should be excitedly expecting them. We should be planning for them because we get to choose the untraveled and often unpaved roads towards a level of self-reflection that can only lead to a life worth living, sharing and experiencing with others. Would we not want that kind of life for ourselves and those we love? Who told us we can no longer have patience, grace and love for ourselves to go into this valley? Somewhere in our lives - WE DID. Guess what, we can again have the power to get us to "the right path" or "the path we should have been on in the first place".

## GOLDEN NUGGET:

Valleys bring blooming flowers so let us welcome them. In every valley, cling to the joy within and find grace for yourself and hold on. Recognize it is healthy to go through the five stages above and to seek professional help, if necessary. Allow yourself to go through the stages, which bring you to the other side of your beautiful flowers.

# DAY TWENTY-ONE

## "Where is the "Social" in Social Media?"

I established a Face Book account a month ago. After three days and 20 friends, I felt a certain way about it. How do you feel about social media? The dictionary provides the following definitions for social:

- *Relating to, devoted to, or characterized by friendly companionship or relations*
- *Seeking or enjoying the companionship of others; friendly; sociable; gregarious*
- *Of, relating to, connected with, or suited to polite or fashionable society*
- *Living or disposed to live in companionship with others or in a community, rather than in isolation*
- *Of or relating to human society, especially as a body divided into classes according to status*

The definitions of media are:

- *A plural of medium. (usually used with a plural verb)*
- *The means of communication, as radio and television, newspapers, magazines, and the Internet, that reach or influence people widely*

Do you agree with these definitions? Most of us would say social media does not represent these things whether it is through the traditional Face Book, Twitter, Instagram, etc., or the recent phenomenon - games or dating apps. These have become another reason to be unauthentic.

We also hide behind our electronics and do not ask for the support when we need it.    If social media truly represented these definitions, it would require all of us to engage consistently and authentically to develop genuine relationships. Until this occurs, social media is more defined as just media for us to create our own show.

**TREASURE:**

None of us can afford not to be present or be connected to those who inspire us to live with genuine connections. We rob ourselves of our human interaction which the social definition above intended. Social is a human interaction. Define who you want to be socially connected, not just through a friend request but through moments that define the journeys you have traveled or want to travel together. The moments you cannot put into words, the tears only you remember, the laughs captured in the bowels of your belly and the joy you have experienced because that person knows the genuine you.

**GOLDEN NUGGET:**

Today, define your purpose for being on social media and the meaning of each connection. Define your boundaries for privacy settings, accepting and rejecting friend requests, and companies and people to follow.  Hopefully, this leaves you with a renewed social media presence.

83

84

# DAY TWENTY -TWO
## Aww Shucks!

How many times have you said, "Aww shucks!" If you didn't say many, as my grandmothers would say, "You are telling a story!" We all have had moments where we could have, should have, but did not. Moments when, we wish things would have been different. Times when, favor was not on our side. In an earlier day, I talked about we cannot rewind or do a "do over" but today I am encouraging us to not stay in the "aww shucks" moments too long. They normally are not valleys of blossoming flowers like the other day, but opportunities to quickly get back on the saddle, in the cockpit, in the runner's track starting command, in the dugout or in the huddle.

When athletes start prematurely from any of these starting positions, it is an "aww shucks" moment but none of them stay there. They quickly get back into the start position. Life is full of premature starts, but we treat them as valleys, excuses or moments for us to not start or try again. Think of all the great athletes who never would have been great if they did not start again.

## TREASURE:

You must give yourself permission to restart at those "aww shucks" moments. Using those "shucks" as opportunities to spring into "action" requires gumption, power, peace, and faith. Action means you are in tune with the joy and greatness within yourself and not phased by crowds around you who are waiting for you to fail, not restart, be fearful and beat yourself up. Your restarts are yours and most times no one is keeping score but you, so…instead of "aww shucks" say let me try that again!

## GOLDEN NUGGET:

How do you feel about restarts? If you have a love/hate relationship, then you probably need to spend some time understanding why. If you feel good about them, then apply Mel Robbins' five second rule from Day 18 and go through the first step of the restart process and keep going! Yeah!!!

# DAY TWENTY-THREE
## "Procrastination Paralysis"

Oh boy! Procrastination is my best friend most days, not because I cannot move forward or complete a task but because I am afraid; I might not meet my own high expectation. YAASS! My own expectations as a Virgo are always incredibly inhuman. There is no wonder my favorite superhero is X-Men Jean because she has all powers hence fewer mistakes, but if you have seen any X-Men movie you know Jean made plenty mistakes and her powers caused quite a bit of chaos. There have been many times when after I have completed a task or moved forward, I have said why did I wait so long to start. For this reason, I added paralysis after procrastination.

When you do not start, you cannot finish, measure where you have been and evaluate how you got there. What if we could begin to use more realistic and positive expectations or outcomes instead of the superhuman ones we often put on ourselves? We begin to look at even the goals that did not turn out so well as solid wins. These wins help frame our future expectations and give us the space to become vulnerable to trying new things more willingly, to erase the superhuman goals and block the perfectionist tendencies that build from being afraid to fail or create something imperfect. As we learned in a previous day, failure sparks self-reflection that we should embrace more.

## TREASURE:

We all feel good about checking items off our task list. It gives us a certain level of achievement and satisfaction. In Day 17, we learned lists do not reflect our long-term goals mainly because we do not take the time to fill them with the things, we want every day, such as changes, restarts, joy, and happiness. Instead, we create lists by doing a mind dump and pushing through them on autopilot. If we start with more realistic, human and positive expectations for the items on our lists, we will not create unachievable tasks or projects. Our lists now become what we truly want and can successfully achieve. We will also attack procrastination with a sincere intention to never allow it to partner with paralysis again.

## GOLDEN NUGGET:

Get some crayons or colored pencils/pens. Now, select your most recent selfie, glue it to your vision board and under it write the characteristics of the new hero - YOU! None of the characteristics can be inhuman or unsustainable.

This hero does not set unrealistic goals or lists. Every day when you look at your vision board these characteristics will serve as your reminder.

# DAY TWENTY-FOUR
## Own Your Affirmations and Compliments

How many of us enjoy affirmations or compliments? Do you know anyone does not like being appreciated or recognized? I heard recently in a church sermon compliments are rarely given for consistent results but more frequently given for quick results. The difference between the two are when you are consistent, credibility becomes your brand. When you are quick, credibility becomes someone who must constantly be validated and praised by others. Building your credibility and a personal brand should be consistent with who you want to be when no one is looking.

It should be personal not detachable so when you do not feel like it you can take it off, put on something else or slow it down. When credibility is given you are always looking for outside affirmations for who you are not when everyone is looking. Sounds exhausting - IT IS! Pretty soon you are questioning your identity. If credibility is not personal, when the affirmations or compliments stop, you are always trying to reach for the next quick fix to receive them.

## TREASURE:

Credibility is earned not given. Live your best life with a personal goal to be who you are at all times, when there are no affirmations or compliments. Consistency illustrates hard work, resilience and perseverance. When credibility is earned, affirmations or compliments come from within and in the energy from everyone and everything you touch. Be credible with yourself first and everyone else will follow suit - perception is always reality. God's perception of us is, *"I will praise thee; for I am fearfully and wonderfully made; marvelous are thy works; and that my soul knoweth right well."* Psalm 139:14 NKJV

## GOLDEN NUGGET:

Let us create a personal brand statement with your own affirmations. You can use the questions – Who are you? What are you good at and why would someone pay you for it? What blessings to others do you create with your brand? Is it a gift or a talent? Gifts are normally extraordinary, for example spiritual extraordinary gifts are the word of wisdom, the word of knowledge, increased faith, the gifts of healing, the gift of miracles, prophecy, the discernment of spirits, diverse kinds of tongues, and interpretation of tongues. Talents are something you have worked hard to master and become skillful but may not be sustainable.  Lasting brands are gifts or core competencies in business language. Now write your personal brand statement, condense it to 30 seconds and practice it with a friend at a networking event or in the mirror each morning.  This is who you are when no one else is looking so be him/her every day.

# DAY TWENTY-FIVE
## Your No's are Also Blessings

Throughout life, we often do not move forward with decisions until after a family member or close friend affirms it, God or some other higher power gives direction, the universe gives us a sign or plans line up just like we want. What decision do we make when none of this happens? We doubt everything leading up to that moment. We ask ourselves what we may have done wrong. We beat ourselves up with so many questions such as why me? Why not me? Instead what if the no's are also yes. It is hard to believe some closed paths are actually open ones. Sometimes the no's are ways of giving us a pause in our tapestry of life to actually choose a future yes. Romans 8:28 [KJV] is one of my favorite bible verses. *"And we know that all things work together for good to them that love God, to them who are the called according to his purpose".* A verse I have come to appreciate and internalize as part of my daily joy and peace.

**TREASURE:**

No's give us a good reason to exit with power. No's also are sometimes doors of grace towards the plan made just for you. Embrace the no's as much as you embrace the yes's because they have a place in your "ultimate" life puzzle too.

**GOLDEN NUGGET:**

In Day 19, remember what you wrote down as your joy within. Romans 8:28 means no matter what happens you remember this joy because the good and bad and the yes's and no's are part of His divine plan for your life. Enjoy all of them.

# CHAPER TWENTY-SIX
## Success …   FULL

We are conditioned to think success looks a certain way. However, when success comes, we do not feel successful because it was always someone else's definition of success. We attach our worth, our goals, our abilities, our treasures, and our greatness to that picture of success. When we are living in someone else's picture and it is shattered, we also think our worth, goals, abilities, and treasures are shattered too.  We often find ourselves lost and confused trying to pick-up the pieces. Pieces that are unfamiliar because they were never ours. The question then is can you create a new picture with no pieces, build new pieces or borrow pieces from others? Creating a new picture to have our own success…FULL life is exciting.  It is fulfilling to have a life built upon a picture of the people, things and experiences we created. Owning your picture gives you the courage to be present in your own life.

**TREASURE:**

Pictures are always full and finished.  No one ever calls an unfinished picture a masterpiece.  If we spend our entire lives holding someone else's picture there will come a time when that picture will also feel unfinished. Being success...FULL means creating your own masterpiece, which gives you the freedom to re-arrange the pieces at your leisure and whenever you want. The freedom to wake-up every day to live your own success is the best picture you will ever create.

**GOLDEN NUGGET:**

Vision boards tell others a lot about who we are, our hopes and dreams and now our hero characteristics. Share your vision board with someone you love who is not afraid to tell you the truth to see if they think it is your masterpiece. Be open to their comments and questions, but most of all be willing to write down any discrepancies in areas they do not easily identify with who they know you to be. Review these discrepancies, make any board changes to reflect your masterpiece and for any remaining discrepancies ensure you are comfortable they truly reflect who you are and make further adjustments.

# DAY TWENTY-SEVEN
## Ride the Waves

As Buddha said, "Pain is temporary, and suffering is optional." Suffering comes from the story that you make up about the pain". This pain is temporary because we learned in Day 25 to accept that all things happen for our good eventually.  Thus, we should brace ourselves, get ready for the ride and throw our hands up in the air.  Those of us who ride roller coasters know pain is what happens every time we get ready to take off.  During the ride our adrenaline is flowing, our hearts are pumping faster, and our mind is focused.  After the ride, we feel so exhilarated, excited, refreshed and sometimes encouraged because we made it again.  Similarly, we should approach our life lessons - head on, with vigor and without fear or regret.  Riding life's waves determines your altitude and mental well-being.  Find something that keeps you focused on what is most important and looking for the next wave.

**TREASURE:**

As Buddha also said, "In the end only three things matter: how much you loved, how gently you lived, and  how gracefully you let go of things not meant for you." Riding the waves gives you the opportunity to take advantage of each one.  You must be willing to seize them.

**GOLDEN NUGGET:**

Create a mantra to remind yourself to ride the waves when pain comes so you forego suffering.  Some may think you are crazy to not wallow in your pain, but I hope you remember this mantra gives you the power to not give away your joy. We have talked a lot about love and living well but we have only spent a little time in letting go, which is the next day… so get ready.

# DAY TWENTY-EIGHT
## Surrender

Yesterday, we discovered how to ride the waves as a contribution from a conversation with my youngest daughter. Today, we are exploring surfing. I love water so thank you for going along with my analogies.

Surfing is a surface water sport in which the wave rider, referred to as a surfer, rides on the forward or face of a moving wave, which usually carries the surfer towards the shore. Life brings so many surprises which have us unprepared, scared and most of all lost, at times. Surfers feel like this every ride. If they do not surrender to the wave, they will fall off or lose their balance which decreases their core muscle's ability to control the board.

If you ask a surfer to describe the experience, they tell you they love the feeling of letting go and being one with the board. Surfers are not surprised by the waves. They do not stop and think about whether they are prepared. They do not abandon the board. They do not question the accuracy of the weather report. They ride THEIR wave embracing their pace, experience, passion, body strength, vision and ability. If they crash, they get right back on the board and try again to reach the shore.

What if we responded to life like surfers respond to the waves?  We would embrace every wave in our life knowing we will eventually get to the shore with more experience.

**TREASURE:**

Surfing reminds us to look at the unexpected occurrences in life as opportunities to pull in our abdominal muscles, stand up straight and surrender.  Why do we need to know where the unexpected waves will take us, how we will get there, will we get there, or even will we be able to use the skills we have used on previous surfs? Can we be satisfied with the hope of getting back to the shore? Sometimes surfs are going to be longer, harder, and scarier than previous ones. Each surf gives you the opportunity to master your ability to surrender to your life and not miss out on a great ride. Embracing each surf leads to a greater freedom…a greater you.  Life is full of low and high waves, winds, and water strength but I know I can do all things through Christ who strengthens me. He goes before me. He prepares my path. He leads me to victory. So, I choose every day to ride the wave and complete my course.

## GOLDEN NUGGET:

Using the mantra from yesterday, pick a daily time when you are going to meditate for 10 minutes. Start slowly by repeating this mantra over and over again for just 10 minutes. Focus on the stillness in your breathing and the way you say the mantra. Meditation frees our mind from racing thoughts and the tendency to want to control in this analogy … you surrender to your own stillness - the surf.

# DAY TWENTY-NINE
## Pictures Tell it All

Yesterday, surrendering to the surf felt so amazing! I thought about what if pictures could capture every moment we surrendered to life. Yes, some of them would not be too flattering but the one thing they would be is genuine. My dad has always loved cameos. Although everyone around him hates them, he is great at taking them because he captures our freedom in the pictures. Imagine today if everyone only posted their cameo shots on social media, what would happen? Everyone would see our vulnerable moments, our blemishes and our loss of control.

Today we do not want others to see these things in our lives, but if we had a photo to look back on; I think we would see the best sides of ourselves that we keep hidden, polished, and photoshopped. We would see our freedom and resilience when we let go and let life happen. We would see so many of our good moments. Some of my best pictures are cameos taken by my dad and loved ones. They are when I am laughing, helping someone, singing or just resting. There is one consistency - they are moments when I was deep in a wave of my life and only the people close to me knew, funny right?

## TREASURE:

Why do we not welcome our best captured uncomfortable, difficult and uncontrollable moments especially if they remind us of the moments when we landed on the shore okay? We need to realize these are the moments that often define our greatest accomplishments or growth. We haven't fallen off the board, our abdominal core is right, and the shore is up ahead. No matter how we look at it, life is full of change, waves, unpredictable surfs, difficult and unexpected moments. They are part of life so we must embrace the waves, look at them differently and get prayed up for the journey to what always leads to a greater us.

## GOLDEN NUGGET:

Create more cameos in your life. Throw away the selfie stick and just take the pic already - you are looking fabulous and a cameo is the best way to remind ourselves that we rode the wave well!!!!! Stop posing for your pics. Every day mentally snap a pic of something that reminds you of the beauty of your best surfed shores.

# DAY THIRTY
## Start Over

In this devotional, I hope you have learned more about yourself. I am certain you also saw some things you recognized from old traditions, what your parents/grandparents said, how society thinks things should happen, and just the no's everyone has told you are not cool. Well given it is the last day and it is time to turn the page, I am thinking we should throw out all of those old traditions and start over with our own. Every day we have a choice to control every moment of our life or to let life happen to us. Unfortunately, many of us are living unhappy lives because we have tried to control too much of our lives. Yet, as we have learned throughout this book when we let life happen to us, we experience more of genuine emotions and unchartered paths trying to get our attention.

These times are more in sync with who we are and what is in store for us as long as we are open to receive them. By being open to receive life, enjoying it becomes more routine and more of the life we want.  We let go of old traditions, thoughts or actions which are no longer relevant, realistic or even reasonable in our family or society. We give ourselves permission to start over each day knowing there is something great in it for us, even the things we least expected or even wanted.

## TREASURE:

The beauty of starting over is you are not burdened by yesterday, the future or even the moments leading up to this decision. You are given a chance to get back at the start line of your race every day to restart the life you choose.  You can enjoy the best parts of this life daily not just when you go on vacation, get a new job, experience a new milestone, find a new partner/spouse, buy a new personal article of clothing, go into a new city/state/country or get a promotion. As a result, you are more apt to allow others to take more cameos of you not waiting to live…but living NOW!!!!

## GOLDEN NUGGET:

Decide today to Live Now, for you. Are you holding on to any old traditions, thoughts and moments from your parents, relatives, friends, or society which are

holding you back from living now? Write them down one by one on a separate sheet of paper and throw them in the trash so you cannot pull them back out again. It is your decision … now that you have so many golden nuggets to guide you and wipe away your excuses, what will you do? If you need to call a friend to help you make this decision, do it. Just live now! Your life is waiting!

# GOLDEN NUGGETS:
Thirty Days of Living Now


**DAY 1:** Make a list of people, places, or situations that make you feel bad or uncomfortable. Determine which ones you want to work through towards being the best you.

**DAY 2:** Buy a gratitude journal and write down the thing you are grateful for today, pause for yesterday and something you will pause for tomorrow.

**DAY 3:** Schedule time on a regular basis to spend with those you love.

**DAY 4:** Pick at least one or two things or places and one or two people you want to do something special with at least once per quarter.

**DAY 5:** Annually, create a list of your loved ones, when you met them, and at least one thing that makes them special and tell them in a handwritten note.

**DAY 6:** For the people who regularly fill your cup take the time to write or call them on a consistent basis or schedule time to watch a movie or TV show together.

**DAY 7:** Quarterly, do your own start, stop and continue exercise to see how many of them create opportunities for you to live now.

**DAY 8:** Practice being open to the human experience everyday by laughing more and write down any areas you need to improve to laugh more.

**DAY 9:** Every six months, review your personal, professional and family plan for flexibility and for God to help you adjust. Make any necessary changes.

**DAY 10:** Write down your level of movement – high, medium, or low and make any changes to increase your silence.

**DAY 11:** By creating a family tree and spending time with family, get to know your organic family to understand how to have better overall wellness.

**DAY 12:** By creating a family tree and spending time with family, get to know your non-organic family to understand how to have better overall wellness.

**DAY 13:** Surrender and do, think or feel what you have been delaying.

**DAY 14:** Remind someone of the basic everyday joy in life and how it can cause any circumstance to take their mind to a place of gratitude and peace.

**DAY 15:** Annually, create a vision board. Look at the vision board every day and ask yourself, what needs to be on the list today? What can I do to water it?

**DAY 16:** Every day select areas of your vision board which do not give you the grace to make room for happiness and joy.

**DAY 17:** At least quarterly, write down what makes you happy. Now compare this list to your vision board and make any changes. Daily, add happy faces to these items.

**DAY 18:**  Pick something you need to change.  Do it, write down how you felt and celebrate with a loved one.

**DAY 19:**  Write down your joy "within" in your gratitude journal.

**DAY 20:**  During every valley, cling to your joy "within", find grace for yourself and commit to the journey.

**DAY 21:**  Create your social media charter – purpose, the meaning of each connection and boundaries (privacy settings, friend requests, and following).

**DAY 22:**  Pick something you need to restart.  Do it, write down how you felt and celebrate with a loved one.

**DAY 23:**  Annually, glue your most recent selfie to your vision board and write the human or sustainable characteristics that make you YOUR own hero.

**DAY 24:**  Create a personal brand statement with your own affirmations and update as necessary.

**DAY 25:**  Remember and recite your joy "within" to get you through the bad times and the "no's" too.

**DAY 26:**  Annually, let someone you love, review your vision board for authenticity.  Make any necessary updates.

**DAY 27:**  Create a mantra to remind yourself to ride the waves when pain comes so you forego suffering.

**DAY 28:**  Schedule a daily time to meditate and repeat your mantra for 10 min.

**DAY 29:**  Create more cameos in your life by capturing the pre-selfie moments.

**DAY 30:**  Write down any old tradition, thought and moment holding you back from living now and throw it away.

# ABOUT THE AUTHOR

Shontelle Mixon is a spiritual success coach, strategic and servant leader and CEO of Just A Sprinkled Filled Purpose, Making Impossibilities Possible. As a CPA, she has over 25 years of accounting/finance and operations experience and has been recognized as an authentic, passionate and emerging thought leader. She is known for her ability to spur growth, transform and realign goals with purpose and conceive and implement strategies that protect, accumulate and preserve what's important at the right time. In May 2019, she was recognized by the Securities Training Corporation as one of the best moms in the financial services industry for her genuine desire and ability to help many small businesses, individuals and families realize what's important to them in their journey for securing holistic wellness.

She is an active member of her alumni chapters of the University of Illinois at Urbana-Champaign and Northwestern University (Kellogg School of Management), Alpha Kappa Alpha Sorority, Inc, The Concilio Board, Great

Girls Network - Chicago and Texas and Big Brothers Big Sisters. She is also an alumni member of both the Leading Women Executives and Leadership Women America. She loves to travel, exercise, read, spend time with her girls, family and friends and helping others. She resides with her two daughters in Frisco, Texas.

# REFERENCES


1.  Braider, Jessica, "Why Is Your Family Dinner So Important?", The Scramble.com, March 30, 2019. Pg.13
2.  Diebel, Matthew, "Eating at Your Desk? Your Cubemates May Be Seething, USA Today, April 6, 2017. Pg.13
3.  Drago, Emily, "The Effect of Technology on Face-to-Face Communication", Elon University - Spring 2015. Pg.14
4.  "Family Reunion Planning Guide", Grouptravel.org. Pg.14
5.  Walsh, Kathryn, "Importance of Family Reunions", USA Today, May 7, 2018. Pg.14